Making Out in Korean

Revised Edition

by Peter Constantine
revised by Gene Baik

D0972822

WITHDRAWN

TUTTLE Publishing

Tokyo | Rutland, Vermont | Singapore

Published by Tuttle Publishing, an imprint of Periplus Editions (HK) Ltd.

www.tuttlepublishing.com

Copyright @ 1995 Peter Constantine
Copyright @ 2004 Periplus Editions (HK) Ltd.
All rights reserved.

LCC Card No. 94061452
ISBN 978-0-8048-3510-7

Distributed by:

North America, Latin America & Europe
Tuttle Publishing
364 Innovation Drive
North Clarendon, VT 05759-9436, USA
Tel: 1 (802) 773 8930
Fax: 1 (802) 773 6993
info@tuttlepublishing.com
www.tuttlepublishing.com

Japan
Tuttle Publishing
Yaekari Building 3F
5-4-12 Osaki, Shinagawa-ku
Tokyo 1410032, Japan
Tel: (81) 3 5437 0171
Fax: (81) 3 5437 0755
sales@tuttle.co.jp
www.tuttle.co.jp

Asia Pacific
Berkeley Books Pte Ltd
61 Tai Seng Avenue #02-12
Singapore 534167
Tel: (65) 6280 1330
Fax: (65) 6280 6290
inquiries@periplus.com.sg
www.periplus.com

14 13 12 11 10   14 13 12 11 10 9

Printed in Singapore

Contents

Introduction

Making Out in Korean introduces a colloquial form of spoken Korean, which you would not learn at any formal language course. It gives you an edge when maneuvering through the ins and outs of everyday life in Korean.

Unlike English, Korean has several speech levels that are formally codified. Age, social standing or the degree of intimacy you have with the person being addressed determines the level of politeness you should adopt. The different speech levels are marked by the verb endings placed at the end of sentences. Needless to say, you are required to use the polite form with strangers, your seniors and to those of a higher social status. However as your relationship with them develops, a more relaxed and casual form of the language may be adopted.

Making Out in Korean presents the intimate and colloquial speech level of Korean that is often used among very close friends including couples. This book contains "street-Korean" in addition to derogatory and vulgar expressions to enrich your spoken Korean!

Apart from the "Curses and Insults" section, any words requiring caution are marked and coupled with explanations to avoid misuse. Although most of this phrase book adopts an intimate and colloquial style of speech, selected expressions are presented in the polite (informal) form, when necessary, and are marked in brackets. The polite (informal) form of Korean is achieved by attaching **-yo** at the end of intimate speech forms, which usually end in **-a** or **-eo**.

Care should be taken not to jump the gun before a relationship has matured. Using an informal or vulgar speech level in the wrong social context would be considered extremely insulting to a Korean person. To be on the safe side, refrain from adopting such levels of speech until the other party initiates it or both parties have reached a mutual agreement to do so.

Basic Grammar

The Korean language follows the word order of Subject-Object-Verb as opposed to the word order (Subject-Verb-Object) of English. Verbs are placed at the end of sentences, a position that reflects its importance in Korean grammar.

I am going to school.	*hak-kkyo ga.* (Statement)
학교 가.	*hahk-kkyo gah.*
Literally means "School go."	

Another salient feature of spoken Korean is that any element of the sentence may be omitted except the verb as long as you can clearly gather from the context what is being talked about. As a result, a single verb can be a complete sentence in Korean as indicated by the third example below.

Go to school!	*hak-kkyo ga!* (Command)
학교 가.	*hahk-kkyo gah!*
Literally means "School go."	

Let's go to school.　　　　*hak-kkyo ga.* (Suggestion)
학교 가.　　　　　　　　　　*hahk-kkyo gah.*
Literally means "School go."

Are you going?　　　　　*ga?* (Question)
가?　　　　　　　　　　　　　*gah?*
Literally means "Go?"

Going to school! (You're joking!)
학교 가!　　　　　　　　　*hak-kkyo ga.* (Exclamation)
　　　　　　　　　　　　　hahk-kkyo gah.

In Korean, the same sentence structure can be used for both sentences and statements. The following examples illustrate that by merely substituting the question word "where" with "school" changes a question into a declarative statement:

Where are you going?　　*erdi ga?* (Question)
어디 가?　　　　　　　　　*erdee gah?*
Literally means "Where go?"

I am going to school.　　*hak-kkyo ga.* (Statement)
학교 가.　　　　　　　　　*hahk-kkyo gah.*
Literally means "School go."

Expressions in the intimate form of speech can be converted into the polite (informal) form by simply adding **-yo** at the end, which usually end in **-a** or **-eo**:

학교 가.　　　　　　*hak-kkyo ga.* (Intimate level of speech)
　　　　　　　　　hahk-kkyo gah.
Literally means "School go."

학교 가요.   **hak-kkyo gayo.**
                     (Informal polite level of speech)
                     hahk-kkyo gahyo.
Literally means "School go."

Reading Romanized Korean

Two systems are used to show the pronunciation of the Korean phrases in the ordinary English alphabet.

The upper line on the right of the page follows the official Revised Romanization of Korean prepared and authorized by the Korean government in 2000. The letters used in this transcription have to be pronounced in a certain way only: they should not be treated like the letters in English which have different sounds in different words, for example the *a* in 'apple,' 'father,' 'syllable' and 'date.'

Because it can at first be quite difficult for English speakers to read romanized Korean correctly, an approximate phonetic equivalent, designed to reflect the closest English equivalent to each Korean sound, is given in a second line underneath the official transcription of each phrase. Where necessary, a hyphen (-) is used to mark a syllable boundary so that any confusion in pronunciation is avoided.

Each phrase is also written in Korean script immediately under the English equivalent on the left of the page, so that if you have difficulty in making yourself understood by following the romanized versions you can show the book to the person you're talking to and they will be able to read what you mean.

Consonants

(1) Simple consonants

ㄱ *g,k*	ㄴ *n*	ㄷ *d,t*	ㄹ *r,l*	ㅁ *m*	ㅂ *b,p*
ㅅ *s*	ㅇ *ng*	ㅈ *j*	ㅊ *ch*	ㅋ *k*	ㅌ *t*
ㅍ *p*	ㅎ *h*				

(2) Double consonants

ㄲ *kk*   ㄸ *tt*   ㅃ *pp*   ㅆ *ss*   ㅉ *jj*

Most of the consonants are pronounced as in English except the tensed (double) consonants.

Double Consonants

There isn't much problem pronouncing romanized Korean except the tensed (double) consonants that require a relatively strong muscular effort in the vocal organs without the expulsion of air.

English	*Korean*	*Approximate in English*
kk	ㄲ	as in "s**k**i," "s**k**y"
tt	ㄸ	as in "s**t**eak," "s**t**ing"
pp	ㅃ	as in "s**p**eak," "s**p**y"
ss	ㅆ	as in "**s**ea," "**s**ir"
jj	ㅉ	as in "bri**dge**," "mi**dg**et" (similar to a tutting sound in an exhaling way)

Vowels

(1) Simple vowels

ㅏ *a*	ㅓ *eo*	ㅗ *o*	ㅜ *u*	ㅡ *eu*	ㅣ *i*
ㅐ *ae*	ㅔ *e*			

(2) Diphthongs

ㅑ *ya*　ㅕ *yeo*　ㅛ *yo*　ㅠ *yu*　ㅒ *yae*　ㅖ *ye*
ㅘ *wa*　ㅙ *wae*　ㅝ *wo*　ㅞ *we*　ㅢ *ui*　ㅚ *oe*
ㅟ *wi*

English	Korean	Approximate in English
a (ah)	ㅏ	as in "**fa**ther"
eo (er)	ㅓ	as in "**tur**d"
o (aw)	ㅗ	as in "f**a**ll"
u (oo)	ㅜ	as in "b**oo**"
eu (oh)	─	as in "tak**e**n"
i (ee)	ㅣ	as in "s**ee**"
ae (a)	ㅐ	as in "t**a**d"
e (e)	ㅔ	as in "b**e**g"
oe (we)	ㅚ	as in "**we**lcome"
ya (yah)	ㅑ	as in "**ya**rn"
yeo (yaw)	ㅕ	as in "**yo**nder"
yo (yo)	ㅛ	as in "**yo**gurt" (said with a slight pull)
yu (yu)	ㅠ	as in "**yu**le" (said with a slight pull)
yae (ya)	ㅒ	as in "**ya**k"
ye (ye)	ㅖ	as in "**ye**s"
wa (wah)	ㅘ	as in "**wi**pe" (first vowel sound of the word; rhymes with "bah")
wae (wa)	ㅙ	as in "**wa**x"
wo (wo)	ㅝ	as in "**wo**nderful"
wi (wi)	ㅟ	as in the "**wee**d"
ui (ooe)	ㅢ	this is a combination of 2 sounds *u* as in "p**u**ll" followed by ee as in "s**ee**."

The Korean writing system, Han-geul (한글)demands that any **written** syllable must begin with a consonant sign. This means that even when a syllable begins with a vowel sound (the syllable contains no spoken consonants) you have to start the syllable with the zero consonant O, which has no sound.

a (ah) 아	*u (oo)* 우	*ae (a)* 애
eo (er) 어	*eu (oh)* 으	*e (e)* 에
o (aw) 오	*i (ee)* 이	*oe (we)* 외

What's Up? **1**

POLITE GREETINGS

How are you?
안녕하세요 ?

annyeonghaseyo?*
ahn-nyawng-hah-seyo?

I'm fine, thanks. And you?
네, 안녕하세요 ?

ne, annyeonghaseyo?
ne, ahn-nyawng-hah-seyo?

Annyeonghaseyo? 안녕하세요? is a greeting that asks about the other person's well-being or good health. This expression can be used at any time of the day as "Good morning," "Good afternoon," "Good evening," "Hi," "Hello," or "How's it going?" The common response is simply *ne, annyeonghaseyo?* 네, 안녕하세요?.

How do you do?

처음 뵙겠습니다.

cheo-eum boep-kket-
 sseumnida.
cher-ohm bwep-kket-ssohm-nee-dah.

What's new?
별일 없지요?

byeollil eop-jjiyo?
byawlleel erp-jeeyo?

—Nothing much.
그저 그래요.

geujeo geuraeyo.
goh-jer goh-rayo.

—Things are hard.
좀 힘들어요.

jom himdeureoyo.
jawm heem-dohr-eryo.

—Things are busy.
좀 바빠요.

jom bappayo.
jawm bah-ppah-yo.

How have you been?
요즘 어떻게 지내세요?

yojeum eotteoke jinaeseyo?
yo-johm ertter-ke jeena-seyo?

—I've been fine, thanks.
잘 지내요.

jal jinaeyo.
jahl jeenayo.

CASUAL GREETINGS BETWEEN CLOSE FRIENDS

How are you doing?
잘 있었어?

jal isseosseo?
jahl eess-ersser?

Yo, what's up?
야, 잘 있었냐?

ya, jal isseonnya?
yah, jahl eess-ernnyah?

Dude, what's up?
새끼, 잘 있었냐?

saekki, jal isseonnya?
sakkee, jahl eess-ernnyah?

자식, 잘 있었냐?

jasik, jal isseonnya?
jah-seek, jahl eess-ernnyah?

*****Saekki** "baby animal" and **jasik** "human baby" are used in Korean slang the way "asshole" is used in American English. When said to one's closest friends, they can be expressions of affection – but handle with care.

How've you been?
어떻게 지냈어?

eotteoke jinaesseo?
ertterke jee-nasser?

—I'm fine.
잘 있었어.

jal isseosseo.
jahl jee-nasser.

Have you been doing OK?
잘 지냈어?

jal jinaesseo?
jahl jee-nasser?

—**Yeah, man!**   *geurae, i jasiga!*
그래, 이 자식아!   *gohra, ee jahseegah!*

Handle with care.

Where did you go?   *eodi gasseosseo?*
어디 갔었어?   *er-dee gahsser-sser?*

It's been a while.   *oraenmaniya.*
오랜만이야.   *awran-mahnee-yah*

—**Yeah!**   *geurae!*
그래!   *goh-ra!*

—**Yeah, it's been ages.**   *geurae, oraenmaniya.*
그래, 오랜만이야.   *goh-ra, awran-mahnee-yah.*

How's Peter/Mary?   *Peter/Mary jal isseo?*
피터 / 메리 잘 있어?   *Peter/Mary jahl eeser?*

—**Yeah, Peter/Mary is fine.**   *eung, (Peter/Mary) jal isseo.*
응, (피터 / 메리) 잘 있어.   *ohng, (Peter/Mary) jahl eesser.*

The subject is often omitted when it is clearly understood from the context.

How are Peter and Mary?   *Peter hago Mary jal isseo?*
피터하고 메리 잘있어?   *Peter hah-gaw Mary jahl eesser?*

—**Yeah, Peter and Mary are fine.**   *eung, (Peter hago Mary) jal isseo.*
응,(피터하고 메리)잘 있어.   *ohng, (Peter hah-gaw Mary) jahl eesser?*

Anything new with Peter/Mary?   *Peter/Mary byeollil eopseo?*
피터 / 메리 별일 없어?   *Peter/Mary byawllell erpser?*

—**Yeah, he/she's doing fine.**   *eung, byeollil eopseo.*
응, 별일 없어.   *ohng, byawlleel erpser.*

—Yeah, he/she's OK.
응, 잘 지내.

eung, jal jinae.
ohng, jahl jeena.

—Yeah, he/she's doing so-so.
응, 그저 그래.

eung, geujeo geurae.

ohng, goh-jer goh-ra.

What's wrong, man?
왜 그래, 임마?

wae geurae, imma?

Handle with care.

wa goh-ra, eem-mah.

—Nothing's wrong with me.
아무것도 아니야.

amugeot-tto aniya.

ahmoogert-taw ahnee-yah.

What are you doing here?
어쩐 일이야?

eojjeon iriya?
erjjern eereeyah?

—Nothing special.
그냥.

geunyang.
goh-nyahng.

Really?
정말?

jeongmal?
jerng-mahl?

Are you serious?
진짜?
jinjja?
jeen-jjah?

Oh, yeah?
그래?
geurae?
goh-ra?

You're lying!
거짓말!
geojinmal!
ger-jeen-mahl!

Are you lying?
거짓말이지?
geojinmariji?
gerjeen-mahree-jee?

Don't lie!
거짓말 마!
geojinmal ma!
gerjeen-mahl mah!

Stop lying!
거짓말 하지 마! 그만 해!
geojinmal haji ma! geuman hae!
ger-jeen-mahl hahjee mah!
   goh-mahn ha!

What?
뭐?
mwo?
mwo?

Huh?
어?
eoh?
erh?

I don't believe it!
믿을 수 가 없어!
mideul su ga eopseo!
meed-ohl soo gah erpser!

Why?
왜?
wae?
wa?

Why not?
왜 아니야?
wae aniya?
wa ah-nee-yah?

You're joking!
농담이지!
nongdamiji!
nawng-dahmee-jee!

You're not joking?
농담 아니지?
nongdam aniji?
nawng-dahm ahnee-jee?

I'm not joking.
농담 아니야.

nongdam aniya.
nawng-dahm ahnee-yah.

He/She's joking!
농담이겠지!

nongdamiget-jji!
nawng-dahm-eeget-jjee!

**Are you making fun
   of me?**
놀리냐?

nollinya?
nawllee-nyah?

I guess so.
그렇겠지.

geureoket-jji.
goh-rerket-jjee.

Maybe.
그럴 거야.

geureol kkeoya.
goh-rerl kkeryah.

Maybe not.
아닐 거야.

anil kkeoya.
ah-neel kker-yah.

That's impossible.
말도 안 돼!

maldo an dwae!
mahl-daw ahn dwa!

You can't do that.
그렇겐 못 해.

geureoken motae.
goh-rerken mawta.

I don't care.
상관 안 해.

sang-gwan an hae.
sahng-gwahn ahn ha.

It's got nothing to do with me.
나랑 상관 없어.

narang sang-gwan eopseo.

nah-rahng sahng-gwahn erpser.

I'm not interested.
관심 없어.

gwansim eopseo.
gwahn-seem erpser.

I think that's it.
그거야.

geugeoya.
goh-ger-yah.

I think this is it.
이거야.

igeoya.
ee-ger-yah.

You're crazy!
너 미쳤어!

neo micheo-sseo!
ner mee-cher-sser!

Damn!
제기랄!

jegiral!
je-gee-rah!

That's right.
맞아.

maja.
mahj-ah.

Is this it?
이거야?

igeoya?
ee-ger-yah?

This is it.
이거야.

igeoya.
ee-ger-yah.

Sure.
그럼.

geureom.
goh-rerm.

It's true.
진짜야.

jinjjaya.
jeen-jjah-yah.

I understand.
알았어.

arasseo.
ahrahsser.

No problem.
문제 없어.

munje eopseo.
moonje erpser.

I like it!
좋아!

joa!
jaw-ah!

—Me, too.
나도.

nado.
nahdaw.

OK!
좋아!

joa!
jaw-ah!

알았어!

arasseo!*
ahrahsser!

*Literally means "I know."

Yo!
야!

ya!
yah!

Handle with care.

Great!
좋아!

joa!
jaw-ah!

Literally means "I like it."

I hope so
그러길 바래.

geureogil barae.
gohrer-geel bahra.

It's risky.
위험해.

wieomhae.
wierm-ha.

Cheer up.
힘 내.

him nae.
heem na.

Smile
웃어 봐.

useo bwa.
ooser bwah.

Basic Phrases   2

Yes.	**ne.** (polite)
네.	*ne.*
	eung. (intimate)
응.	*ohng*
No.	**anio.** (polite)
아니오.	*ahneeaw.*
	ani. (intimate)
아니.	*ahnee.*
Right.	**maja.**
맞아.	*mahjah.*
What?	**mwo?**
뭐?	*mwo?*

Who?
누구?

nugu?
noogoo?

Where?
어디?

eodi?
erdee?

When?
언제?

eonje?
ernje?

Why?
왜?

wae?
wa?

How?
어떻게?

eotteoke?
ertterke?

Which?
어떤 거?

eotteon geo?
erttern ger?

Whose?
누구 거?

nugu kkeo?
noogoo kker?

This.
이거.

igeo.
eeger.

That.
저거.

jeogeo. (something over there)
jerger.
geugeo. (something close to the listener)

그거.

gohger.

Here.
여기.

yeogi.
yawgee.

There.
저기.

jeogi. (over there)
jergee.
geogi. (close to the listener)

거기.

gergee.

Maybe.
그럴 거야.

geureol kkeoya.
gohrerl kkeryah.

Maybe not.
아닐 거야.

anil kkeoya.
ahneel kkeryah.

I
나

na
nah

You
너

neo
ner

He/She
쟤

jyae (used in a person's presence)
jya

개

gyae (used in a person's absence)
gya

We
우리

uri
ooree.

You (plural)
너네들

neonedeul
nernee-dohl.

They
쟤네들

jyaenedeul
jyane-dohl

Don't!
하지 마!

haji ma!
hahjee mah!

Please.
제발.

jebal.
jebahl.

Thank you.
감사합니다.
고마워.

gamsahamnida (polite).
gahmsah-hahm-needah.
gomawo (intimate).
gawmahwo.

Can I have this?
이거 가져도 돼?

igeo gajeodo dwae?
eeger gahjer-daw dwa?

How much is this?
이거 얼마예요?

igeo eolmayeyo? (polite)
eeger erlmah-yeyo?

That's not cheap.
싼게 아니예요.

ssan ge anieyo. (polite)
ssahn ge ahneeeyo.

That's too expensive!
너무 비싸요!

neomu bissayo! (polite)
nermoo bee-sahyo!

I'm not buying this.
이거 안 살 거예요.

igeo an sal kkeoyeyo. (polite)
eeger ahn sahl kkeryeyo.

**Make it cheaper and
   I'll buy it.**
좀 더 싸면 살게요.

jom deo ssa-myeon salkkeyo.
(polite)
jawm der ssah-myawn sahl-kkeyo.

Got a Minute? 3

One moment.
잠깐만 기다려.

jamkkanman gidaryeo.
jahm-kkahn-mahn geedah-ryaw.

When?
언제?

eonje?
ernje?

Till when?
언제까지?

eonje kkaji?
ernje kkahjee?

What time?
몇 시에?

myeot-ssie?
myawt-sseee?

Am I too early?
나 너무 일찍 왔지?

na neomu iljjik wat-jji?
nah nermoo eeljjeek waht-jjee?

Is it too late?
너무 늦었지?

neomu neujeot-jji?
nermoo nohjert-jjee?

When is it good for you?
언제가 좋아?

eonjega joa?
ernjegah jaw-ah?

What time is good for you?
몇 시가 좋아?

myeot-ssiga joa?
myawt-ssee-gah jaw-ah?

How about later?
나중에 어때?

najung-e eottae?
nahjoong-e ertta?

How about tomorrow?
내일 어때?

naeil eottae?
naeeel ertta?

How about the day after tomorrow?
모레 어때?

more eottae?

mawre ertta?

When can I come?
나 언제 가도 돼?

na eonje gado dwae?
nah ernje gahdaw dwa?

When can we go?
우리 언제 갈 수 있어?

uri eonje gal su isseo?
ooree ernje gahl soo eesser?

What time do we arrive?
우리 몇 시에 도착해?

uri myeot-ssie dochake?
ooree myawt-sseee daw-chahke?

What time will we be back?
우리 언제 쯤 돌아 와?

uri eonje jjeum dora wa?
ooree ernje jjohm dawrah wah?

Are you ready?
준비됐어?

junbi dwaesseo?
joonbee dwasser?

When will you do it?
언제 할 거야?

eonje hal kkeoya?
ernje hahl kkeryah?

When will you be done?
언제 끝낼 수 있어?

eonje kkeunnael su isseo?
ernje kkohn-nal soo eesser?

How long will it take?
얼마나 걸려?

eolmana geollyeo?
erlmah-nah gerllyaw?

—It'll be done soon.
금방 될 거야.

geumbang dwoel kkeoya.
gohm-bahng dwwel kkeryah.

Not now.
지금은 안 돼.

jigeumeun an dwae.
jeegoh-mohn ahn dwa.

Before.
그전에.

geujeone.
goh-jerne.

Next time.
다음에.

da-eume.
dah-ohme.

I don't know.
몰라.

molla.
mawllah

I don't know when.
언제 일지 몰라.

eonje iljji molla.
ernje eeljjee mawl-lah.

I don't know now.
지금은 몰라.
jigeumeun molla.
jeegoh-mohn mawl-lah.

I'm not sure.
확실히 몰라.
hwak-ssiri molla.
hwahk-sseeree mawl-lah.

Sometime (later).
다음에.
da-eume.
dah-ohme.

Any time's OK.
아무때나 좋아.
amuttaena joa.
ahmoo-ttanah jaw-ah.

Every day.
매일
maeil.
maeel.

You decide when.
네가 언젠지 결정해.
niga eonjenji gyeoljjeonghae.
neegah ern-jenjee gyawl-jjerng-ha.

Whenever you want.
네가 원하는 곳으로 해.
niga wonhaneun goseuro hae.
neegah won-hahnohn gawsoh-raw ha.

OK, let's meet then.
그럼, 그때 만나.
geureom, geuttae manna.
gohrerm, gohtta mahnnah.

Let's go!
가자!
gaja!
gahjah!

Let's go for it.
한 번 해 보자.
han beon hae boja.
hahn bern ha bawjah.

Hurry up.
빨리빨리.
ppalli ppalli.
ppahllee ppahllee.

Let's start again.
다시 하자.
dasi haja.
dahsee hahjah.

Let's continue.
계속하자.
gyesokaja.
gyesaw-kahjah.

Yeah!
야!

ya!
yah!

I'll do it quickly.
빨리 할게.

ppalli halkke.
ppah-lee hahl-kkee.

I'll finish soon.
금방 끝낼게.

geumbang kkennaelkke.
gohm-bahng kken-nalkke.

Finished?
끝났어?

kkeunnasseo?
kkohn-nahsser?

—I'm finished.
끝났어.

kkeunnasseo.
kkohn-nahsser.

Hey There! 4

Listen to what I'm saying! *ne mal jom deureobwa!*
내 말 좀 들어 봐! *ne mahl jawm dohrerbwah!*

Listen to him/her. *jyae mal jom deureobwa.*
쟤 말 좀 들어 봐. *jya mahl jawm dohrerbwah.*

Listen to them. *jyaenedeul mal jom deureobwa.*
쟤네들 말 좀 들어 봐. *jyan-edohl mahl jawm dohrerbwah.*

Did you hear me? *nae mal deureosseo?*
내 말 들었어? *na mahl dohr-ersser?*

Can you hear me? *nae mal deullyeo?*
내 말 들려? *na mahl dohl-lyaw?*

Literally means "Can you hear my voice clearly?"

Do you understand? *arasseo?*
알았어? *ahr-ahsser?*

Do you understand, or not? *arasseo, mollasseo?*
알았어, 몰랐어? *ahr-ahsser, mawl-lahsser?*

Can you understand me? *nae mal iaehae?*
내 말 이해해? *na mahl eeaha?*

—I don't understand. *iaega an dwae.*
이해가 안 돼. *eeagah ahn dwa.*

I didn't understand. *jal mollasseo.*
잘 몰랐어. *jahl mawl-lahsser.*

I couldn't understand.
이해할 수 가 없었어.
iaehal ssu ga eopseosseo.
eeahahl ssoo gah erps-ersser.

What?
뭐?
mwo?
mwo?

What did you say?
뭐라고 했어?
mworago haesseo?
mwo-rahgaw hasser?

**I don't understand what
   you're saying.**
무슨 말인지 모르겠어.
museun marinji moreugesseo.
*moo-sohn mahr-eenjee
   mawroh-gesser.*

Don't say such things.
그런 말 하지 마.
geureon mal haji ma.
gohrern mahl hahjee mah.

You shouldn't say things like that.
그런 말은 하면 안 돼.
geureon mareun hamyeon an dwae.
gohrern mahrohn hah-myawn ahn dwa.

Did you say that?
네가 그랬어?
niga geuraesseo?
neegah goh-rasser?

You said that, right?
네가 그랬지?
niga geuraet-jji?
neegah gohrat-jjee?

I didn't say that.
난 그런 말 한 적 없어.
nan geureon mal han jeok eopseo.
nahn gohrern mahl hahn jerk erpser.

I didn't say anything.
난 아무말도 안 했어.
nan amumaldo an haesseo.
nahn ahmoo-mahldaw ahn hasser.

I didn't tell anyone.
아무한테도 말 안 했어.
amuhantedo mal an haesseo.
ahmoo-hahntedaw mahl ahn-hasser.

Let's speak Korean!
한국말로 하자!
han-gungmallo haja!
hahn-goong-mahllaw hahjah!

Literally means "Let's do it in Korean."

Can you speak Korean?
한국말 하세요?
han-gungmal haseyo? (polite)
hahn-goong-mahl hahseyo?

한국말 할 수 해?
han-gungmal hae? (intimate)
hahn-goong-mahl ha?

Let's talk.
얘기 좀 하자.
yaegi jom haja.
yagee jawn hahjah.

Let's talk more.
조금만 더 얘기하자.
jogeumman deo yaegihaja.
jawgohm-mahn der yagee-hahjah.

Let's talk later.
이따가 얘기하자.
ittaga yaegihaja.
eettah-gah yagee-hahjah.

Tell me later.
이따가 얘기해 줘.
ittaga yaegihae jwo.
eettahgah yageeha jwo.

I don't want to talk.
얘기하고 싶지 않아.
yaegihago sip-jji ana.
yagee-hahgaw see-jjee ahnah.

**I don't want to talk
with you.**
너랑 얘기하고 싶지 않아.
neorang yaegi hago sip-jji ana.
*ner-rahng yagee hahgaw seep-jjee
ahnah.*

**I don't want to hear
about it.**
그런 말 듣고 싶지 않아.
*geureon mal deut-kko sip-jji
ana.*
*gohrern mahl doht-kkaw seep-jjee
ahnah.*

**I don't want to hear about
that thing.**
그 얘긴 듣고 싶지 않아.
geu yaegin deut-kko sip-jji ana.
*goh yageen doht-kkaw seep-jjee
ahnah.*

Don't make excuses!
변명하지 마!
byeonmyeonghaji ma!
byawn-myawng-hahjee mah!

Don't give me excuses!
핑계 따윈 듣고 싶지 않아!
*pinggye ttawin deut-kko sip-jji
ana!*
*peeng-gye ttah-ween doht-kkaw
seep-jjee ahah!*

Stop complaining.
불평 좀 하지 마.
bulpyeong jom haji ma.
bool-pyawng jawm hahjee mah.

Don't talk so loud.
너무 크게 말하지 마.
neomu keuge malhaji ma.
nermoo kohge mahl-hahjee mah.

Speak up.
크게 말해 봐.
keuge malhae bwa.
kohge mahlha bwah.

Speak louder.
더 크게 말해 봐.

deo keuge malhae bwa.
der kohge mahlha bwah.

Say it again.
다시 말해 봐.

dasi malhae bwa.
dahsee mahlha bwah.

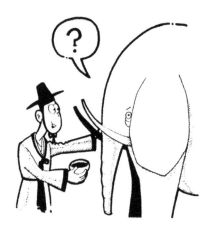

Look at That! 5

Look!
봐!

bwa!
bwah!

Look at this!
이거 좀 봐!

igeo jom bwa!
eeger jawm bwah!

Don't look!
보지 마!

boji ma!
bawjee mah!

Don't look at this/that!
이거 / 저거 보지 마!

igeo/jeogeo boji ma!
eeger/jerger bawjee mah!

Can you see it?
보여?

boyeo?
bawyaw?

—I can see it clearly.
잘 보여.

jal boyeo.
jahl bawyaw.

—I can't see it.
잘 안 보여.

jal an boyeo.
jahl ahn bawyaw.

Did you see that?
저거 봤어?

jeogeo bwasseo?
jerger bwahsser?

Did you see it?
그거 봤어?

geugeo bwasseo?
gohger bwahsser?

—I saw it.
그거 봤어.

geugeo bwasseo.
gohger bwahsser.

—I didn't see it.
그거 못 봤어.

geugeo mot bwasseo.
gohger mawt bwahsser.

I don't want to see it.
보고 싶지 않아.

bogo sip-jji ana.
bawgaw seep-jjee ahnah.

Did you see Jinju?
진주 봤어?

Jinju bwasseo?
jeenjoo bwahsser?

I want to see you soon.
나 너 빨리 보고 싶어.

na neo ppalli bogosipeo.
nah ner ppahllee bawgaw-seeper.

Are you going to meet Junju soon?
진주 곧 만날 거야?

Jinju got mannal kkeoya?

jeenjoo gawt mahnnahl kkeryah?

—I'm going to meet Junju soon.
진주 곧 만날 거야.

Jinju got mannal kkeoya.

Jeenjoo gawt mahnnahl kkeryah.

Did you meet John?
존 만났어?

John mannasseo?
John mahn-nahsser?

—I met John.
존 만났어.

John mannasseo.
John mahn-nahsser.

Well, we meet again.
어, 또 만나네.

eo, tto mannane.
er, ttaw mahn-nahne.

Coming and Going

6

Come here!
이리 와!

iri wa!
eeree wah!

Come over here!
이리로 와!

iriro wa!
eereeraw wah!

Come later.
나중에 와.

najung-e wa.
nahjoong-e wah.

Can you come?
올 수 있어?

ol ssu isseo?
awl ssoo eesser?

Come with me.
나랑 같이 가.

narang gachiga.
nah-rahng gah-cheegah.

He/She's coming here.
개 여기 올 거야.
gyae yeogi ol kkeoya.
gya yawgee awl kkeryah.

They are coming here.
개네들 여기 올 거야.
gyaenedeul yeogi ol kkeoya.
gyane-dohl yawgee awl kkeryah.

I'll go soon.
곧 갈 거야.
got gal kkeoya.
gawt gahl kkeryah.

I'll come over soon.
곧 갈게.
got galkke.
gawt gahlkke.

I can go.
갈 수 있어.
gal ssu isseo.
gahl ssoo eesser.

I think I can go.
갈 수 있을 거 같애.
gal ssu isseul geo gatae.
gahl ssoo eessohl ger gahta.

I can't go.
못 가.
mot-kka.
mawt-kkah.

I want to go.
나 가고 싶어.
na gago sipeo.
nah gahgaw seeper.

Do you want to go?
너 가고 싶어?
neo gago sipeo?
ner gahgaw seeper?

Do they want to go?
개네들 가고 싶어해?
gyaenedeul gago sipeohae?
gya-nedohl gahgaw seeper-ha?

I want to go to Seoul.
나 서울가고 싶어.
na seoul gago sipeo.
nah serool gahgaw seeper.

I really want to go.
나 정말 가고 싶어.
na jeongmal gago sipeo.
nah jerng-mahl gahga seeper.

I don't want to go.
나 가고 싶지 않아.
na gago sip-jji ana.
nah gahgaw seep-jjee ahnah.

I really don't want to go.
나 정말 가고 싶지 않아.

na jeongmal gago sip-jji ana.
nah jerng-mahl gahgaw seep-jjee ahnah.

You're going, right?
너 갈 거지?

neo gal kkeoji?
ner gahl kkerjee?

I'm going.
나 갈 거야.

na gal kkeoya.
nah gahl kkeryah.

I'm not going.
나 안 갈 거야.

na an gal kkeoya.
nah ahn gahl kkeryah.

I didn't go
나 안 갔어.

na an gasseo.
nah ahn gahsser.

Don't go!
가지 마!

gaji ma!
gahjee mah!

Don't go yet!
아직 가지 마!

ajik gaji ma!
ahjeek gahjee mah!

I have to go.
나 지금 가야 돼.

na jigeum gaya dwae.
nah jee-gohm gahyah dwa.

I must go now.
나 지금 꼭 가야 돼.

na jigeum kkok gaya dwae.
nah jee-gohm kkawk gahyah dwa.

May I go?
나 가도 돼?

na gado dwae?
nah gahdaw dwa?

I'm going/leaving.
나 간다.

na ganda.
nah gahndah.

Shall we go?
우리 갈까?

uri galkka?
ooree gahlkkah?

Let's go!
가자!

gaja!
gahjah!

Let's get outa here!
나가자!

nagaja!
nah-gahjah!

Let's split!
흩어지자!

heuteojija!
hohter-jeejah!

He/She left.
걔 떠났어.

gyae tteonasseo.
gya tter-nahsser.

Stay here!
여기 있어!

yeogi isseo!
yawgee eesser!

Where are you going?
너 어디 가?

neo eodi ga?
ner erdee gah?

Go slowly.
천천히 가.

cheoncheoni ga.
chern-chernee gah.

Eat, Drink, Be Merry!

7

I'm hungry.
나 배고파.

na baegopa.
nah bagaw-pah.

I'm starving.
배고파 죽겠어.

baegopa juk-kkesseo.
bagaw-pah jook-kkesser.

Literally means "I'm dying from hunger; I'm going crazy from hunger."

Have you eaten?
너 밥 먹었어?

neo bap meogeosseo?
ner bahp merg-ersser?

—I haven't eaten yet.
아직 안 먹었어.

ajik an meogeosseo.
ahjeek ahn merg-ersser.

Do you want to eat something?
뭐 좀 먹을래?

mwo jom meogeullae?

mwo jawm merg-ohlla?

I'd like to eat something.
나 뭐 좀 먹고 싶어.

na mwo jom meok-kko sipeo.
nah mwo jawm merk-kkaw seeper.

Do you want some more?
더 먹을래?

deo meogeullae?
der merg-ohlla?

I'm thirsty.
나 목말라.

na mongmalla.
nah mawng-mahllah.

I want to drink some beer.
나 맥주 마시고 싶어.

na maek-jju masigo sipeo.
nah mak-jjoo mah-seegaw seeper.

I want some liquor.
나 술 마시고 싶어.

na sul masigo sipeo.
nah sool mah-seegaw seeper.

Try some ... (beverage)
... 좀 마셔 봐.

... jom masyeo bwa.
... jawm mahsyaw bwah.

Korean vodka
소주

soju
sawjoo

Mild, milky rice liquor
막걸리

mak-kkeolli
mahk-kkerllee

Beer
맥주

maek-jju
mak-jjoo

Wine
포도주

podoju
pawdaw-joo

Plum wine
매실주

maesiljju
massel-jjoo

This tastes too weird.
맛이 신기해.

masi sin-gihae.
mahsee seen-geeha.

I think this has gone bad.
이거 상한 거 같애.

igeo sang-han geo gatae.
eeger sahng-hahn ger gahta.

I think this stuff's stale.
이거 맛이 간 거 같애.

igeo masi gan geo gatae.
eeger mahsee gahn ger gahta.

Literally means "This taste has left."

Wow! This tastes good!
와! 맛있다.

wa! masit-tta!
wah! mahseet-ttah!

More, more!
더, 더!

deo, deo!
der, der!

**Do you want to drink
  some more?**
더 마실래?

deo masillae?

der mah-seella?

**—Thank you, but I still
  have plenty.**
아니, 아직 많이 남았어.

ani, ajik mani namasseo.
*ahnee, ahjeek mahnee
  nahm-ahsser.*

**Come on, dude, have
  some more!**
그러지 말고 더 마셔, 임마!

*geureoji malgo deo masyeo,
  imma!*
*gohrer-jee mahlgaw der mahsyaw,
  eemmah!*

Handle the expression with care.

It's on me!
내가 낼게!

naega naelkke!
nagah nalkke!

Literally means "I'll pay!"

How about some food?
밥 먹고 싶어?

bap meok-kko sipeo?
bahp merk-kkaw seeper?

Is the food ready?
밥 준비 다 됐어?

bap junbi da dwaesseo?
bahp joonbee dah dwasser?

—Yeah, it's ready.
응, 다 됐어.

eung, da dwaesseo.
ohng, dah dwasser.

This is a feast!
진수성찬이네요!

jinsuseongchanineyo!
jeen-sooserng-chahnee-neyo!

A formulaic phrase used when one is invited for dinner.

Try this!
이거 좀 먹어 봐!

igeo jom meogeo bwa!
eeger jawm merger bwah!

Try that!
저거 좀 먹어 봐!

jeogeo jom meogeo bwa!
jerger jawm merger bwah!

Dude, stuff your face!
임마, 빨리 먹어!

imma, ppalli meogeo!
eemmah, ppahl-lee merger!

Handle the expression with care.

That looks delicious.
맛있겠다.

masit-kket-tta.
mahseet-kket-ttah.

Wow, it looks delicious!
와, 맛있겠다!

wa, masit-kket, tta!
wah, mahseet-kket, ttah!

Oh, that smells good!
야, 냄새 좋다!

ya, naemsae jota!
yah, namsa jawtah!

What's this?
이거 뭐야?

igeo mwoya?
eeger mwoyah?

Taste it.
맛 좀 봐.

mat jom bwa.
maht jawm bwah.

What's it called?
이거 이름이 뭐야?

igeo ireumi mwoya?
eeger eerohmee mwoyah?

Is it hot? (spicy)
매워?

maewo?
mawo?

This is boiling!
뜨거워!

tteugeowo!
ttohgerwo!

Yuck!
으윽!

eueuk!
ohohk!

It tastes like shit!
맛이 지랄 같애!

masi jiral gatae!
mahsee jeerahl gahta!

It's awful!
맛 없어!

madeopseo!
mahderpser!

I can't eat this!
못 먹겠어!

monmeok-kkesseo!
maw-nmerk-kkesser!

Water, water!
물, 물!

mul, mul!
mool, mool!

My tongue's on fire!
입에서 불난다!

ibeseo bullanda!
eebeser boollahn-dah!

How'd you eat this?
이거 어떻게 먹어?

igeo eotteoke meogeo?
eeger ertterke merger?

Are these chopsticks?
이거 젓가락이야?

igeo jeot-kkaragiya?
eeger jert-kkahrahg-eeyah?

Give me a fork.
포크 줘.

pokeu jwo.
pawkoh jwo.

You want a knife?
칼 줄까?

kal julkka?
kahl jool-kkah?

Have some *bulgogi.*
불고기 좀 먹어 봐.

bulgogi jom meogeo bwa.
bool-gawgi jawh merger bwah.

* Sweet and savory stir-fried beef.

I'd like to try some
  boshingtang.*
나 보신탕 먹어 보고 싶어.

na bosintang meogeo bogo sipeo.
bool-gawgi jawh merger bawgaw seeper.

* Dog-meat stew.

Careful, that *tteokbokki*
  is hot!
조심해, 떡볶이 매워!

josimhae, tteok-ppokki maewo!

jaw-seemha, tterk pawkkee mawo.

* Rice cake mixed with hot chilly paste and vegetables.

That's a dip, don't drink it!

찍어 먹는 거야, 마시지 마!

jjigeo meongneun geoya, masiji ma!

jjeeger merng-nohn gerya, mah-seejee mah!

Give me some.
나 좀 줘.

na jom jwo.
nah jawn jwo.

Give me a little more.
조금 더 줘.

jogeum deo jwo.
jaw-gohm der jwo.

You want more food?
더 먹을래?

deo meogeullae?
der mer-gohlla?

—I'd like more food.
나 더 먹을래.

na deo meogeullae.
nah der mer-gohlla.

Enough?
훙분해?

chungbunae?
choong-boona?

—Enough!
훙분해.

chungbunae.
choong-boona.

I Like it!

8

I like this.
나 이거 맘에 들어.

좋아.

I like that.

나 저거 맘에 들어.

좋아.

na igeo mame deureo. (objects)
nah eeger mahme dohrer.
***joa.** (non objects)*
jaw-ah.

na jeogeo mame deureo.
(objects)
nah jerger mahme dohrer.
***joa.** (non objects)*
jaw-ah.

I really like that!
나 그거 정말 좋아!

na geugeo jeongmal joa!
nah gohger jerng-mahl jaw-ah!

I don't like that.
나 그거 싫어.

na geugeo sireo.
nah gohger seerer.

I don't really like it.
나 그거 별로야.

na geugeo byeolloya.
nah gohger byawl-lawyah.

No, thanks.
괜찮아요.

gwaenchanayo. (polite)
gwan-chahn-ahyo

됐어요.

dwaesseoyo. (polite)
dwasseryo

괜찮아.

gwaenchana.
gwan-chahnah.

됐어.

dwaesseo.
dwasser.

Gwaenchanayo and its more casual version *gwaenchana* mean "It's OK,"
while *dwaesseoyo* and the casual *dwaesseo* mean "It's done."

I want ...
나 ... 할래.

na ... hallae.
nah ... hahlla.

This
이거

igeo
eeger

That
저거

jeogeo (something over there)
jerger

*geugeo (something close to
the listener)*

그거

gohger

I want ... (used with nouns)
나 ... 갖고 싶어.

na ... gat-kko sipeo.
nah ... gaht-kkaw seeper.

**I don't want ... (used with
nouns)**
나 ... (갖기) 싫어.

na ... (gat-kki) sireo.

nah ... (gaht-kkee) seerer.

A computer
컴퓨터

keompyuteo
kerm-pyuter

A camera
카메라

kamera
kahmerah

A radio
라디오

radio
rahdeeaw

A video recorder
비디오

bidio
beedeeaw

A tape
테입

teip
teeep

TV
티비

tibi
teebee

CD
시디

ssidi
sseedee

An MD
엠디

emdi
emdee

A mobile phone
휴대폰

hyudaepon
hyuda-pawn

A laptop computer
노트북

noteubuk
nawtoh-book

I don't need that.
나 그거 필요 없어.

na geugeo piryo eopseo.
nah gohger peeryo erpser.

I don't need this.
나 이거 필요 없어.

na igeo piryo eopseo.
nah eeger peeryo erpser.

I'm busy.
나 바빠.

na bappa.
nah bahppah.

I'm happy.
나 행복해.

na haengbokae.
nah hang-bawka.

I feel good.
나 기분 좋아.

na gibun joa.
nah gee-boon jaw-ah.

I'm glad to know that.
알려줘서 고마워

allyeo jwoseo gomawo.
ahl-lyaw jwoser gaw-mahwo.

I'm sad.
나 슬퍼.

na seulpeo.
nah sohlper.

I'm fine.
나 괜찮아.

na gwaenchana.
nah gwan-chahnah.

I'm afraid.
나 무서워.

na museowo.
nah moo-serwo.

I'm getting sick of it!
지겨워.

jigyeowo!
jee-gyawwo!

I'm irritated!
짜증나!

jjajeungna!
jjah-johngnah!

Man, I'm irritated!
에이, 짜증나!

ei, jjajeungna!
eee, jjah-johngnah!

I'm confused!
뭐가 뭔지 모르겠어!

mwoga mwonji moreugesseo!
mwogah mwonjee mawroh-gesser!

Literally means "I don't know which is which."

I'm going crazy.
나 미치겠어.

na michigesseo.
nah meechee-gesser.

I'm pissed off!
나 열 받았어!

na yeol badasseo!
nah yawl bahd-ahsser!

I'm mad! (angry)
나 화났어!

na hwanasseo!
nah hwah-nahsser!

I'm ready.
나 준비 다 됐어.

na junbi da dwaesseo.
nah joon-bee dah dwasser.

I'm sleepy.
나 졸려.

na jollyeo.
nah jawllyaw.

I'm tired.
나 피곤해.

na pigonae.
nah peegawna.

I'm wasted.
나 갔어.

na kasseo.
nah kahsser.

Literally means "I left!;" too much alcohol, too many parties…

I'm totally wasted!
나 완전히갔어!

na wanjeoni gasseo!
nah wahn-jernee gahsser!

I'm out of it!
머리가 빙빙 돌아.

meoriga bingbing dora!
mer-reegah beeng-beeng dawra!

My head's going "ping!" i.e., it's spinning.

I'm bored!
심심해!

simsimae!
seem-seema!

I feel sick.
나 아파.

na apa.
nah ahpah.

I'm disappointed.
나 실망했어.

na silmanghaesseo.
nah seel-mahng-hasser.

I'm disappointed in you.
나 너한테 실망했어.

na neohante silmanghaesseo.
nah nerhahnte seel-mahng-hasser.

What a drag!
아, 따분해!

ah, ttabunae!
ahh, ttah-boona!

Oh, god! (How awful!)
세상에!

sesang-e!
sesahng-e!

What a pity!
참 안 됐다!

cham an dwaet-tta!
chahm ahn dwat-ttah!

Can you do it?
너 할 수 있어?

neo hal ssu isseo?
ner hahl ssoo eesser?

—I can do it.
나 할 수 있어.

na hal ssu isseo.
nah hahl ssoo eesser.

—I can't do it.
나 못 해.

na motae.
nah mawta.

Sorry, I can't do it.
미안하지만, 안 되겠어.

mianhajiman, an doegesseo.
meeahn-hahjee-mahn, ahn dawe-gesser.

Sorry.
죄송합니다.

joesonghamnida. (polite)
jawe-sawng-hahmneedah.
mianae.
meeahna.

미안해.

I can't believe it.
믿을 수 가 없어.

mideul ssu ga eopseo.
meedohl ssoo gah erpser.

I'll do it.
내가 할게.

naega halkke.
nagah hahlkke.

I know.
알고 있어.

algo isseo.
ahlgaw eesser.

I know him/her.

나 쟤 알아.

na jyae ara. (used in person's
        presence)
nah jya ahrah.
na gyae ara. (used in person's
        absence)

나 걔 알아.

nah gya ahrah.

Do you know that?
너 그거 알아?

neo geugeo ara?
ner gohger ahrah?

Oh, you know that.
너 그거 알잖아.

neo geugeo aljana.
ner gohger ahljah-nah.

I don't know.
나 몰라.

na molla.
nah mawllah.

I'll think about it.
좀 생각해 볼게.

jom saenggakae bolkke.
jawm sang-gahka bawlkke.

I'm so confused.
너무 헷갈려.

neomu het-kkallyeo.
nermoo het-kkahllyaw.

I made a mistake.
실수했어.

silssuhaesseo.
seelssoo-hasser.

Am I right?
내가 맞아?

naega maja?
nagah mahjah?

Am I wrong?
내가 틀려?

naega teullyeo?
nagah tohllyer?

Curses and Insults

9

What do you want?
뭐야?

mwoya?
mwoyah?

What do you want, asshole?
뭐야, 임마?

mwoya, imma?
mwoyah, eemmah?

What?
뭐?

mwo?
mwo?

What you lookin' at?
뭘 봐?

mwol bwa?
mwol bwah?

Anything wrong?
꼽냐?

kkomnya?
kkawm-nyah?

You givin' me attitude?
어쭈, 째려 봐?

eojju, jjaeryeo bwa?
erjjoo, jjaryaw bwah?

Literally means "Why are you looking down on me?"

What are you staring at?
뭘 쳐다 봐?

mwol cheoda bwa?
mwol cherdah bwah?

—None of your business.
남이야.

namiya.
nahm-eeyah

Literally means "Other person." The idea is: "That is the kind of question you could ask yourself, but I'm not you — so it's none of your business!"

Mind your own business.
참견하지 마.

chamgyeonhaji ma.
chahm-gyawhahjee mah.

Go away!
꺼져!

kkeojeo!
kkerjer!

Go away, man!
꺼져, 임마!

kkeojeo, imma!
kkerjer, eem-mah!

Fuck off!
좆까!

jot-kka!
jawt-kkah!

Literally means "Kick penis!" From *jot*, "penis," and *kka*, "kick."

Excuse me?
뭐?

mwo?
mwo?

What did you just say?
방금 뭐라고 했어?

banggeum mworago haessec?
bahng-gohm mwo-rahgaw hasser?

Do you know who I am?
내가 누군지나 알아?

naega nugunjina ara?
nagah noogoon-jeenah ahrah?

Come here, I'll teach you some manners!
싸가지 없는 새끼야,
이리 와!

ssagaji eomneun saekkiya, iri wa!
ssah-gahjee erm-nohn sakkee-ya, eeree wah!

Literally means "You have no manners, baby; come here!"

Come here!
이리 와!

iri wa!
eerree wah!

Don't joke with me!
농담하지 마!

nongdamhaji ma!
nawng-dahm-hahjee mah!

Stop it!
그만 해!

geuman hae!
goh-mahn ha!

Shut up!
입 닥쳐!

ip dakcheo!
eep dahkcher!

What're you doing?
뭐 하는 짓이야?

mwo haneun jisiya?
mwo hah-nohn jee-seeyah?

What'd you hit me for?
왜 쳐?

wae cheo?
wa cher?

What'd you push me for?
왜 밀어?

wae mireo?
wa meerer?

I'm gonna kill you!
너 죽여 버릴 거야.

neo jugyeo beoril kkeoya!
ner joogyaw berreel kkeryah!

Have you finished?
다 끝났어?

da kkeunnasseo?
dah kkoh-nnahsser?

You wanna fight?
맞장 떠?

mat-jjang tteo?
maht-jjahng tter?

We gonna fight, or not?
싸울 거야, 말 거야?

ssaul kkeoya, mal kkeoya?
ssah-ool kker-yah, mahl kker-yah?

Let's fight and see!
한 번 해 보자구!

han beon hae bojagu!
hahn bern ha baw-jahgoo!

Ouch!
아야!

aya!
ahyah!

Don't!
그만!

geuman!
goh-mahn!

That hurts!
아파!

apa!
ahpah!

Help!
사람살려!

saram sallyeo!
sah-rahm sahllyaw!

도와주세요!

dowajuseyo!
daw-wah-jooseyo!

Literally means "Save a person's life!"

Don't hit me!
때리지 마!

ttaeriji ma!
tta-reejee mah!

You deserve it!
맞아도 싸!

majado ssa!
mahj-ahdaw ssah!

Don't do it again!
다신 하지마!

dasin hajima!
dah-seen hah-jeemah!

Say you're sorry!
사과해!

sagwahae!
sahgwah-ha!

—Sorry.
미안해.

mianhae.
mee-ahnha.

You're right.
네가 맞아.

nega maja.
negah mahjah.

I was wrong.
내가 틀렸어.

naega teullyeosseo.
nagah tohl-lyawss-er.

It was my fault.
내가 잘못했어.

naega jalmotaesseo.
nagah jahl-mawtass-er.

Forgive me.
용서해 줘.

yongseohae jwo.
yong-serha jwo.

I forgive you.
용서해 줄게.

yongseohae julkke.
yong-serha joolkke.

You're making me laugh!
웃기네!

ut-kkine!
oot-kkeene!

You win.
네가 이겼어.

niga igyeosseo.
neegah ee-gyawss-er.

I lose.
내가 졌어.

naega jeosseo.
nagah jersser.

SPECIAL KOREAN INSULTS

I'll kick your penis!
좆까!

jot-kka!
jawt-kkah!

You're lower than an insect.
벌레만도 못한 새끼.

beollemando motan saekki.
berlle-mahn-daw mawtahn sakkee.

Son of a beggar.
거지 새끼.

geoji saekki.
gerjee sakkee.

Son of a bitch.
개 새끼.

gae saekki.
ga sakkee.

Son of an idiot.
바보 새끼.

babo saekki.
bahbaw sakkee.

Fuck!
씨발!

ssibal!
sseebahl!

Fuck you!
씨발 놈!

ssibal nom! (to male)
ssee-bahl nawn.

씨발 년!

ssibal nyeon! (to female)
ssee-bahl nyawn!

씨방새!

ssibangsae!
ssee-bahngsa!

You peasant!
쌍년!

ssyangnyeon! (women)
ssyang-nyawn!

쌍놈!

ssyangnom! (men)
ssyang-nawn!

You look like a penis!
좆 같은 놈!

jot-kkateun nom! (men)
jawt-kkaht-ohn nawm!

좆 같은 년!

jot-kkateun nyeon! (women)
jawt-kkaht-ohn nyawn!

Don't show off!
잘난 척 하지마!

jallan cheok hajima!
jahllahn cherk hahjee-mah!

Go drink your mother's breast milk and then come back!
가서 엄마 젖이나 더 먹고 와!

gaseo eomma jeojina deo meok-kko wa!

gahser erm-mah jerj-eenah der merk-kkaw wah!

Go home and masturbate!
집에 가서 딸딸이나 쳐!

jibe gaseo ttalttarina cheo!
jeebe gahser ttahl-ttahr-eenah cher!

Are you insane?
왠 지랄이야?

waen jirariya?
wan jeerahr-eeyah?

Crazy man!
미친 놈!

michin nom!
mee-cheen nawn!

Crazy woman!
미친 년!

michin nyeon!
mee-cheen nyawn!

Ah, stupid!
아, 멍청한 새끼!

ah, meongcheong-han saekki!
ahh, merng-cherng-hahn sakkee!

Dickhead!
돌대가리!

dolttaegari!
dawltta-gahree!

Pig!
지저분한 새끼!

jijeobunan saekki!
jeejer-boonahn sakkee!

Bad-luck-woman!
재수 없는 년!

jaesu eomneun nyeon!
jasoo erm-nohn nyawn!

Bad-luck-man!
재수 없는 새끼!

jaesu eomneun saekki!
jasoo erm-nohn sakkee!

Oh, I lost my appetite!
아, 밥 맛 없어!

ah, bammat eopseo!
ahh, bahm-maht erpser!

Implies that the person being insulted is so unseemly that the speaker's stomach is turning.

Pervert!
변태 새끼!

byeontae saekki!
byawnta sakkee!

You're a dirty man.
더러운 새끼.

deoreo-un saekki.
derrer-oon sakkee.

You're a dirty woman.
더러운 년.

deoreo-un nyeon.
derrer-oon nyawn!

Oh, shit smell!
아, 너저분한 새끼!

ah, neojeobunhan saekki!
ahh, nerjer-boon-hahn sakkee!

Die!
뒈져 버려!

dwejeo beoryeo!
dwejer berryer!

**Why don't you go
    somewhere and die!**
어디 가서 뒈져 버려!

eodi gaseo dwejeo beoryeo!

erdee gahser dwejer berryaw!

What a fucking mess!
아, 씹할 좃 같네!

ah, ssipal jot-kkanne!
ahh, sseep-ahl jawt-kkahn-ne!

You motherfucker!
니미 씹할 놈!

nimi ssipal nom!
neemee sseep-ahl nawm!

Damn!
씨발!

ssibal!
ssee-bahl!

Bastard!
호로 새끼!

horo saekki!
hawraw sakkee!

Wanker!
좆 같은 새끼!

jot-kkateun saekki!
jawt-kkaht-ohn sakkee!

Bitch!
개 같은 년!

gae gateun nyeon!
ga gaht-ohn nyawn!

You piece of shit!
좆도 아닌 새끼!

jot-tto anin saekki!
jawt-ttaw ahneen sakkee!

Party Talk   10

All the expressions in this section are polite speech.

Do you come here often?
여기 자주 오세요?

yeogi jaju oseyo?
yawgee jahjoo awseyo?

You look like you're having fun.
참 재미 있어 보이네요.

cham jaemi isseo boineyo.
chahm jamee eesser bawee-neyo.

—Yes, I'm having fun.
네, 재미 있어요.

ne, jaemi isseoyo.
ne, jamee eess-eryo.

This place is happening!
여기 괜찮다!

yeogi kwaenchanta!
yawgee kwan-chahntah!

—Yeah, this place is happening!
예, 여기 괜찮아요!

ye, yeogi kwaenchanayo!
ye, yawgee kwan-chahn-ahyo!

This place is fun.
여기 정말 재있어요.
yeogi jeongmal jaemisseoyo.
yawgee jerng-mahl jameess-eryo.

This place is fantastic.
여기 멋있어요.
yeogi meosisseoyo.
yawgee merseess-eryo.

What's your name?
이름이 어떻게 되세요?
ireumi eotteoke dwoeseyo?
eerohm-ee ertterke dwoe-seyo?

—My name is ...
제 이름은 ... 입니다.
je ireumeun ... imnida.
je eerohm-ohn ... eem-needa.

Are you here alone?
혼자 왔어요?
honja wasseoyo?
hawn-jah wahss-eryo?

—Yes, I'm here alone.
네, 혼자 왔어요.
ne, honja wasseoyo.
ne, hawnjah wahss-eryo.

—No, I'm here with my ...
아니오, ... 랑 왔어요.
anio, ... rang wasseoyo.
ahnee-aw ... rahng wahsseryo.

Father
아버지
abeoji
ahber-jee

Daddy
아빠
appa
ahppah

Mother
어머니
eomeoni
ermee-nee

Mum
엄마
eomma
erm-mah

Older sister
언니
eonni (female)
ernnee

누나
nuna (male)
noonah

Older brother
오빠

oppa (female)
awppah

hyeong (male)
hyawng

형

Younger sister/brother
동생

dongsaeng
dawng-sang

Friends
친구

chin-gu
cheen-goo

Boyfriend
남자친구

namjachin-gu
nahm-jah-cheen-goo

Girlfriend
여자친구

yeojachin-gu
yaw-jah-cheen-goo

Husband
남편

nampyeon
nahm-pyawn

Wife
아내

anae
ahna

senior
선배

seonbae
sern-ba

junior
후배

hubae
hooba

Can I join you?
합석해도 될까요?

hap-sseokaedo doelkkayo?
hahp-sserka-daw dwel-kkahyo?

Can I sit here?
여기 앉아도 될까요?

yeogi anjado doelkkayo?
yergee ahnjah-daw dwel-kkahyo?

Please sit down.
예, 앉으세요.

ye, anjeuseyo.
ye, ahnjoh-seyo.

Is someone sitting here?
여기 누구 있어요?

yeogi nugu isseoyo?
yawgee noogoo esser-yo?

—Someone's sitting here.
여기 누구 있어요.

yeogi nugu isseoyo.
yawgee noogoo eesser-yo.

Can I buy you a drink?
술 한 잔 사도 될까요?

sul han jan sado doelkkayo?
sool hahn jahn sahdaw
  dwel-kkahyo?

Where are you from?
어디서 왔어요?

eodiseo wasseoyo?
erdeeser wah-sser-yo?

—I'm from ...
저는 ... 에서 왔어요.

jeoneun ... eseo wasseoyo.
jernohn ... eser wah-sser-yo.

the U.S.
미국

miguk
mee-gook

England
영국

yeongguk
yerng-gook

France
프랑스

peurangseu
pohrang-eoh

Australia
호주

hoju
hawjoo

Germany
독일

dogil
daw-geel

Canada
캐나다

kaenada
kanah-dah

Italy
이탈리아

itallia
eetahl-leeah

Russia
러시아

reosia
rerseea

Korea
한국

han-guk
hahn-gook

Japan
일본

ilbon
eebawn

China
중국

jungguk
joong-gook

Hong Kong
홍콩

hongkong
hawng-kawng

Indonesia
인도네시아

indonesia
eendaw-neseeah

Thailand
태국

taeguk
tagook

Where do you live?
어디에 살아요?

eodie sarayo?
erdeee sahr-ahyo?

—I live in ...
... 에 살아요.

... e sarayo.
... e sahrahyo.

New York
뉴욕

nyuyok
nyuyok

L.A.
엘에이

erei
ereee

Seoul
서울

seo-ul
ser-ool

Busan
부산

busan
boo-sahn

London
런던

reondeon
rern-dern

Sydney
시드니

sideuni
see-dohnee

Melbourne
멜번

melbeon
melbern

Paris
파리

pari
pahree

Rome
로마

roma
rawmah

How old are you?
나이가 어떻게 되세요?

naiga eotteoke doeseyo?
nah-eegah ertterke dweseyo?

—I'm ... years old.
... 살이에요.

... sarieyo.
... sahree-eyo.

15
열다섯

yeol daseot
yerl dahsert

16
열여섯

yeol yeoseot
yerl yer-sert

17
열일곱

yeol ilgop
yerl eel-gawp

18
열여덟

yeol yeodeol
yerl yer-derl

19
열아홉

yeo aop
yer ahawp

20
스무

seumu
sohmoo

21
스물한

seumul han
sohmool hahn

22
스물두

seumul du
sohmool doo

23
스물세

seumul se
sohmool se

24
스물네

seumul ne
sohmool ne

25
스물다섯

seumul daseot
sohmool dahsert

26
스물여섯

seumul yeoseot
sohmool yawsert

27
스물일곱

seumul ilgop
sohmool eelgawp

28
스물여덟

seumul yeodeol
sohmool yawderl

29
스물아홉

seuml aop
sohmool ahawp

30
서른

seoreun
ser-rohn

31
서른한

seoreun han
ser-rohn hahn

32
서른두

seoreun du
ser-rohn doo

33
서른세

seoreun se
ser-rohn se

34
서른네

seoreu ne
ser-roh ne

35
서른다섯

seoreun daseot
ser-rohn dahsert

40
마흔

ma-eun
mah-ohn

50
쉰

swin
sween

Are you a student?
학생이세요?

hak-ssaeng-iseyo?
hahk-ssang-eeseyo?

I'm a ...
저는 ... 입니다.

jeoneun ... imnida.
jernohn ... eemnee-dah.

Doctor
의사

uisa
ooeesah

Dentist
치과의사

chikkwa uisa
chee-kkwah ooeesah

Lawyer
변호사

byeonosa
byawnaw-sah

Professor
교수

gyosu
gyosoo

Secretary
비서

biseo
beeser

Teacher
선생

seonsaeng
sernsang

Nurse
간호사

ganosa
gahnaw-sah

Business person
사업가

sa-eopkka
sah-erpkkah

Company employee
회사원

hoesawon
hwe-sahwawn

Public servant
공무원

gongmuwon
gawng-moowawn

Hairdresser
미용사

miyongsa
mee-yongsah

Sales person
영업사원

yeong-eop sawon
yawng-erp sahwawn

Wow, what a nice job you've got!
와, 멋있는 일 하시네요!

wa, meosinneun il hasineyo!
wah, mersee-nnohn eel hahsee-neyo!

What kinds of hobbies do you have?
취미가 어떻게 되세요?

chwimiga eotteoke doeseyo?
chwi-meegah ertterke dweseyo?

—My hobby is ...
제 취미는 ... 입니다.

je chwimineun ... imnida.
je chwi-meenohn ... eem-needah.

Sport
운동

undong
oon-dawng

Tennis
테니스

teniseu
tenee-soh

Golf
골프

golpeu
gawl-poh

Music
음악

eumak
ohmahk

Ballet
발레

balle
bahlle

Cooking
요리

yori
yoree

Fishing
낚시

nak-ssi
nahk-ssee

Skiing
스키

seuki
sohkee

What music do you like?
어떤 음악 좋아해요?

eotteon eumak joahaeyo?
erttern ohmak jawah-hayo?

—I like ...
저는 ... 좋아해요.

jeoneun ... joahaeyo.
jernohn ... jawah-hayo.

You know this song?
이 노래 알아요?

yi norae arayo?
yee nawra ahrahyo?

—Yes, I do.
네, 알아요.

ne, arayo.
ne, ahrahyo.

—I don't know it.
잘 몰라요.

jal mollayo.
jahl mawl-lahyo.

**—This is the first time
I'm hearing it.**
처음 들어요.

cheo-eum deureoyo.

cher-ohm dohreryo.

Would you like to dance?
춤 출래요?

chum chullaeyo?
choom choollayo?

—**I can't dance.**
춤 못 춰요.
chum mot chwoyo.
choom mawt chwoyo.

—**I'm not in the mood.**
춤 출 기분이 아니에요.
chum chul gibuni anieyo.
choom chool geeboon-ee anee-eyo.

You dance well.
춤 잘 추네요.
chum jal chuneyo.
choom jahl chooneyo.

Shall we go elsewhere?
어디 다른 데로 갈래요?
eodi dareun dero gallaeyo?
erdee dahrohn deraw gallayo?

What time do you have to be home?
몇 시까지 집에 가야 돼요?
myeot-ssikkaji jibe gaya dwaeyo?
myawt-sseekkah-jee jeebe gahyah dwayo?

What time are you leaving?
몇 시에 갈 거예요?
myeot-ssie gal kkeoyeyo?
myawt-sseee gahl kkerye-yo?

—**I have to go now.**
지금 가야 돼요.
jigeum gaya dwaeyo.
jee-gohm gahyah dwayo.

Don't go now.
지금 가지 마세요.
jigeum gaji maseyo.
jee-gohm gahjee mahseyo.

Go later!
이따가 가세요!
ittaga gaseyo!
eettahgah gah-seyo!

What shall we do?
뭐 할까요?
mwo hallaeyo?
mwo hahlla-yo?

What's next?
이제 뭐 할까요?
ije.mwo halkkayo?
eeje mwo hahl-kkahyo?

—**It's up to you.**
하고 싶은 대로 하세요.
hago sipeun daero haseyo.
hahgaw seepohn daraw hah-seyo.

Do you wanna come to my place?
우리 집으로 갈래요?

uri jibeuro gallaeyo?

ooree jeeboh-raw gahllayo?

—I'm not sure.
잘 모르겠어요.

jal moreuget-sseoyo.
jahl maw-rohget-sseryo.

Just for coffee.
그냥 커피 마시러 가요.

geunyang keopi masireo gayo.
goh-nyahng kerpee mah-seerer gahyo.

—Yes, let's go.
네, 가요.

ne, gayo.
ne, gahyo.

Getting Serious

11

I want to know more about you.
너에 대해서 더 알고 싶어.
neo-e dae-aeseo deo algo sipeo.
ner-e da-asser der ahlgaw seeper.

Shall we meet again?
우리 또 만날까?
uri tto mannalkka?
ooree ttaw mahn-nahl-kkah?

When can I see you again?
언제 다시 만날 수 있어?
eonje dasi mannal ssu isseo?
ernje dahsee mahn-nahl ssoo eesser?

Can I call you?
내가 전화해도 돼?
naega jeonwahaedo dwae?
nagah jernwah-hadaw dwa?

Will you call me?
나한테 전화할래?
nahante jeonwahallae?
nah-hahnte jernwah-hahlla?

Here's my phone number.
이거 내 전화번호야.
igeo nae jeonwabeonoya.
eeger na jernwah-bernaw-yah.

What's your number?
전화번호가 어떻게 돼?

jeonwabeonoga etteoke dwae?
jernwah-bernaw-gah etterke dwa?

—My phone number is ...
내 전화번호는 ...

nae jeonwabeononeun ...
na jernwah-bernaw-nohn ...

563 – 4718
오육삼 (에) 사칠일팔

o-yuk-sam (e) sa-chil-il-pal
aw-yook-sahm (e)
  sah-cheel-eel-pahl

890 – 1234
팔구공 (에) 일이삼사

pal-gu-gong. (e) il-yi-sam-sa
pahl-goo-gawng (e)
  eel-yee-sahm-sah

1 *il*	**2** *yi*	**3** *sam*	**4** *sa*	**5** *o*
일 *eel*	이 *yee*	삼 *sahm*	사 *sah*	오 *aw*

6 *yuk*	**7** *chil*	**8** *pal*	**9** *g*	**0** *gong*
육 *yook*	칠 *cheel*	팔 *pahl*	구 *goo*	공 *gawng*

What's your e-mail address?
이메일 주소가 어떻게 돼?

imeil jusoga eotteoke dwae?
eeme-eel joo-sawgah ertterke dwa?

— My e-mail address is ...
내 이메일 주소는 ...

nae yimeil jusoneun ...
na yeeme-eel joosaw-nohn ...

It was fun.
재미 있었어.

jaemi isseosseo.
jamee eess-ersser.

On the Phone

12

Hello.
여보세요.

yeoboseyo.
yawbawseyo.

This is Robert. Is Mary at home?
전 로버트인데요,
　메리 집에 있어요?

jeon Robeoteu-indeyo, Mary jibe isseoyo? (polite)
jern Raw-bertoh-eendeyo, Mary jeebe eesseryo?

Mary is out.

메리 어디 나갔는데요.

Mary eodi nagannundeyo.
　(polite)
Mary erdee nah-gahnnoon-deyo.

Wait a minute.

잠깐만 기다리 세요.

jamkkanman gidariseyo.
　(polite)
jahm-kkahn-mahn gee-dah-reeseyo.

Mary! Telephone!
메리! 전화!

Mary! jeonwa!
Mary! jernwah!

It's me, Robert.
나 로버트야.

na Robeoteuya.
nah Raw-bertoh-yah.

What are you doing?
지금 뭐 해?

jigeum mwo hae?
jee-gohm mwo ha?

Shall we meet now?
지금 만날까?

jigeum mannalkka?
jee-gohm mahn-nahl-kkah?

I wanna see you.
나 너 보고 싶어.

na neo bogo sipeo.
nah ner bawgaw seeper.

I can't go out now.
지금 못 나가.

jigeum monnaga.
jee-gohm mawn-nahgah.

I'll call you tomorrow.
내가 내일 전화할게.

naega naeil jeonwahalkke.
nagah naeel jern-wah-hahlkke.

Bye!
잘 있어.

jal isseo!
jahl eesser!

Literally means "Stay well" usually said by the person who called.

—Yes.
응, 그래 !

eung, geurae!
ohng, gohra!

Lovers' Language 13

I love you.
사랑해.

saranghae.
sahrahng-ha.

I'm crazy about you.
난 너가 좋아 미치겠어.

nan neoga joa michigesseo.
nahn nergah jaw-ah meechee-
gesser.

I'm yours.
난 니꺼야.

nan nikkeoya.
nahn nee-kkerya.

You're mine.
넌 내꺼야.

neon naekkeoya.
nern na-kkerya.

You're beautiful.
너 참 예뻐.

neo cham yeppeo. (to women)
ner chahm yepper

You're handsome.
너 참 잘 생겼어.

neo cham jal saenggyeosseo.
    (to men)
ner chahm jahl sang-gyawss-er.

You're sexy.
너 섹시해

neo sek-ssihae.
ner sek-sseeha.

Your ... is/are beautiful.
너 ... 예뻐.

neo ... yeppeo.
ner ... yepper.

Eyes
눈

nun
noon

Lips
입술

ip-ssul
eep-ssool

Hands
손

son
sawn

Face
얼굴

eolgul
erlgool

Legs
다리

dari
dahree

Nose
코

ko
kaw

Breasts
가슴

gaseum
gahsohm

Neck
목

mok
mawk

Shoulder
어깨

eokkae
erkka

Back
등

deung
dohng

Butt
엉덩이

eongdeong-i
ohng-derng-ee

You have a beautiful body.
넌 몸매가 예뻐.

neon mommae-ga yeppeo.
nern maw-mma-gah yepper.

You smell nice.

너한텐 좋은 냄새가 나.

neohanten jo-eun naemsaega na.
ner-hahn-ten jaw-ohn nam-sagah nah.

Can I kiss you?
키스해도 돼?

kiseuhaedo dwae?
keesoh-hadaw dwa?

Kiss me!
키스해 줘!

kiseuhae jwo!
keesoh-ha jwo!

Do you wanna sleep with me?
나랑 자고 싶어?

narang jago sippeo?
nah-rahng jahgaw seeper?

Oh, I'm embarrassed.
아이, 창피해.

ai, changpihae.
ahee, chahng-peeha.

Don't be shy.
부끄러워 하지 마.

bukkeureowo haji ma.
boo-kkoh-rerwo hahjee mah.

Close your eyes.
눈 감아 봐.

nun gama bwa.
noon gahmah bwah.

Turn off the light.
불꺼 봐.

bulkkeo bwa.
bool-kker bwah.

IN THE BEDROOM

Is this your first time?
너 처음이야?

neo cheo-eumiya?
ner cher-ohmeeyah?

Tell me the truth.
사실대로 말해 봐.

sasildaero malhae bwa.
sahseel-daraw mahlha bwah.

I'm still a virgin.
나 아직 처녀야.

나 아직 총각이야.

na ajik cheonyeoya. (female)
nah ahjeek cher-nyawyah.
na ajik chonggagiya. (male)
nah ahjeek chawng-gah-geeyah.

I'm frightened.
무서워.

museowo.
mooserwo.

Don't worry.
걱정하지 마.

geok-jjeonghaji ma.
gerk-jjerng-hahjee mah.

I'll be careful.
조심할게.

josimhalkke.
jaw-seem-hahlkke.

I wanna hold your hand.
너 손잡아 보고 싶어.

neo sonjaba bogo sipeo.
ner sawn-jahbah bawgaw seeper.

Look into my eyes.
내 눈 쳐다 봐.

nae nun cheoda bwa.
na noon cherdah bwah.

Hug me.
나 안아 줘.

na ana jwo.
na ahnah jwo.

Take your ... off!
... 벗어 봐!

... beoseo bwa!
... berser bwah!

Clothes
옷

ot
awt

Jeans
청바지

cheongbaji
cherng-bahjee

Dress
드레스

deureseu
doh-resoh

Skirt
치마

chima
cheemah

T-shirt
티셔츠

tisyeocheu
tee-syaw-choh

Socks
양말

yangmal
yahng-mahl

Sneakers
신발

sinbal
seen-bahl

Shoes
구두

kudu
koodoo

Bra
브라

beura
bohrah

Underwear
팬티

paenti
pantee

The Korean word **paenti**, despite its derivation from the English "panty," is gender-neutral.

I'm cold!
나 추워!

na chuwo!
nah choowaw!

Make me warm.
따뜻하게 해 줘.

ttatteutage hae jwo.
ttahttoh-tahge ha jwo.

Come closer to me.
더 가까이 와.

deo gakkai wa.
der gahkkah-ee wah.

That tickles.
간지러워.

ganjireowo.
gahnjee-rerwo.

IN BED

I wanna see your ...
나 니 ... 보고 싶어.

na ni ... bogo sipeo.
nah nee ... bawgaw seeper.

I wanna touch your ...
나 니 ... 만지고 싶어.

na ni ... manjigo sipeo.
nah nee ... mahn-jeegaw seeper.

I wanna suck your ...
나 니 ... 빨고 싶어.

na ni ... ppalgo sipeo.
nah nee ... ppahlgaw seeper.

Thing
거

kkeo
kker

Breasts
가슴

gaseum
gahsohm

Pussy
보지

boji (derogatory form)
bawjee

거기

geogi (gender neutral)*
gergee

Dick
자지

jaji (derogatory form)
jahjee

거기

geogi (gender neutral)*
gergee

* *Geogi* literally means "there".

Balls
불알

bural
boorahl

Nipples
젖꼭지

jeot-kkok-jji
jert-kkawk-jjee

Butt
엉덩이

eongdeong-i
erng-derng-ee

Knees
무릎

mureup
moo-rohp

Toes
발가락

balkkarak
bahlk-kahrahk

Fingers
손가락

sonkkarak
sawnk-kahrahk

I'm afraid I'll get pregnant.
임신할까 봐 무서워.

imsinhalkka bwa museowo.
*eem-seen-hahl-kkah bwah
mooserwu.*

Use a condom!
콘돔 써!

kondom sseo!
kawn-dawn sser!

**I don't like to wear a
condom.**
콘돔 쓰는 거 싫어.

kondom sseuneun geo sireo.

kawn-dawn ssoh-nohn ger seerer.

**If you don't wear a
condom, I won't do it!**
콘돔 안 쓰면, 안 할꺼야!

*kondom an sseumyeon, an
halkkeoya!*
*kawn-dawn ahn ssoh-myawn,
ahn hahl-kkeryah.*

Oh, it feels so good!
아, 기분 좋아!

ah, gibun joa!
ahh, geeboon jaw-ah!

Touch me!
나 만져 줘!

na manjeo jwo!
nah mahnjer jwo!

Bite me!
깨물어 줘!

kkaemureo jwo!
kka-moorer jwo!

More, more!
조금만 더, 조금만 더!

jogeumman deo, jogeumman deo!
jawgohm-mahn der, jawgohm-mahn der!

Deeper, deeper!
더 깊이, 더 깊이!

deo gipi, deo gipi!!
der geepee, der geepee!

Faster, faster
더 빨리, 더 빨리!

deo ppalli, deo ppalli!
der ppahllee, der ppahllee!

Harder, harder!
더 세게, 더 세게!

deo sege, deo sege!
der sege, der sege!

Wait, wait!
잠깐만, 잠깐만!

jamkkanman, jamkkanman!
jahm-kkahn-mahn, jahm-kkahn-mahn!

I'm coming, I'm coming!
나온다, 나온다!

naonda, naonda! (men)
nah-awndah, nah-awndah!

오를 거 같애!

oreul kkeo gatae! (women)
awrohl kker gahta!

I came.
나 쌌어.

na ssasseo. (men)
nah ssahsser.

나 올랐어.

na ollasseo. (women)
nah awllahsser.

—I know.
알아.

ara.
ahrah.

Did it feel good?
기분 좋았어?

gibun joasseo?
gee-boon jaw-ahsser?

Let's get married.
우리 결혼하자.

uri kyeoronhaja.
ooree kyawr-awn-hahjah.

I wanna be your wife.
네 아내가 되고 싶어.

ni anaega doego sipeo.
nee ahnagah dwegaw seeper.

I wanna be your husband.
네 남편이 되고 싶어.

ni nampyeoni doego sipeo.
nee nahm-pyawnee dwegaw seeper.

I don't want to get married yet.
아직은 결혼하고 싶지 않아.

ajigeun gyeoronhago sip-jji ana.
ahjeegohn gyawrawn-hahgaw seep-jjee ahnah.

I'm too young.
지금은 너무 일러.

jigeumeun neomu illeo.
jee-gohm-ohn nermoo eeller.

Literally means "It's too early."

I'm already married.
나 결혼했어.

na gyeoronhaesseo.
nah gyawrawn-hasser.

I love you, but I can't become your wife/husband.
널 사랑하지만, 네 아내는 / 남편은될 수 없어.

neol saranghajiman, ni anaeneun/nampyeoneun doel ssu eopseo.
nerl sahrahng-hahjee-mahn, nee ahna-nohn/nahm-pyawnohn dwel ssoo erpser.

I need time to think.
생각할 시간이 필요해.

saenggakal sigani piryohae.
sang-gahkahl seegahnee peeryo-ha.

This is so sudden.
너무 갑자기야.

neomu gap-jjagiya.
nermoo gahp-jjah-gee-yah.

We must think about this.

우리 더 생각해 봐야 될 거
같애.

uri deo saenggakae bwaya
*   doel kkeo gatae.*
ooree der sang-gahka bwahyah
*   dwel kker gahta.*

Do you want to come to ...
with me?
나랑 ... 갈래?

narang ... gallae?

nahrahng ... gahlla?

the USA
미국

miguk
meegook

Canada
캐나다

kaenada
kanahdah

Europe
유럽

yureop
yoorerp

Australia
호주

hoju
hawjoo

I want to stay in Korea.
나 한국에 있고 싶어.

na han-guge it-kko sipeo.
nah hahn-googe eet-kkaw seeper.

Farewell 14

Let's not see each other again.
우리 다시는 만나지 말자.
uri dasineun mannaji malja.
ooree dah-seenohn mahn-nahjee mahljah.

I hate you!
너 싫어!
neo sireo!
ner seerer!

Don't call me again.
다신 전화하지 마.
dasin jeonwahaji ma.
dah-seen jernwah-hahjee mah.

Get lost!
꺼져!
kkeojeo!
kkerjer!

Give it up, already.
포기해.
pogihae.
pawgeeha.

I don't love you anymore.
더 이상 널 사랑하지 않아.
deo yisang neol saranghaji ana.
der yee-sahng nerl sah-rahng-hahjee ahnah.

You're boring.
너 재미없어.
neo jaemi eopseo.
ner jamee erpser.

Literally means "You're no fun."

Stop following me.
귀찮게 굴지 마.
gwichanke gulji ma.
gwee-chahnke gooljee mah.

Do you have another lover?
다른 사람 생겼어?
dareun saram saenggyeosseo?
dahrohn sah-rahm sang-gyawsser?

It's my fault.
내가 잘못했어.
naega jalmotaesseo.
nagah jahl-mawtasser.

Can we start again?
다시 시작할 순 없어?
dasi sijak hal sun eopseo?
dahsee seejahk hahl soon erpser?

I can't live without you.
너 없인 살 수 없어.
neo eopsin sal ssu eopseo.
ner erpseen sahl ssoo erpser.

Please understand me.
제발 나 좀 이해해 줘.
jebal na jom iaehae jwo.
jebahl nah jawm ee-aha jwo.

I'll never forget you.
널 잊을 순 없을 거야.
neol ijeul sun eopseul kkeoya.
nerl eejohl soon erpsohl kkeryah.

Can we still be friends?
우리 친구로 지낼 수 있어?
uri chin-guro jinael ssu isseo?
ooree cheen-gooraw jeenal ssoo eesser?

I'll always love you.
널 언제나 사랑할 거야.
neol eonjena saranghal kkeoya.
nerl ern-jenah sahrahng-hahl kkeryah.

I'll miss you.
보고 싶어 질 거야.
bogo sipeo jil kkeoya.
bawgaw seeper jeel kkeryah.

I'll always think about you.
언제나 너 생각할게.
eonjena neo saenggak halkke.
ernjenah ner sang-gahk hahlkke.

I'll call you when I come back.
돌아와서 전화할게.

dorawaseo jeonwa halkke.

dawrah-wahser jern-wah hahlkke.

I'll be back soon.
곧 올게.

got olkke.

gawt awlkke.

Do you have to go?
꼭 가야 돼?

kkok gaya dwae?

kkawk gahyah dwa?

Please don't go!
제발 가지 마!

jebal gaji ma!

jebahl gahjee mah!

Stay here with me.
나랑 같이 여기 있어.

narang gachi yeogi isseo.

nah-rahng gahch-ee yawgee eesser.

I have to go.
나 가야 돼.

na gaya dwae.

nah gahyah dwa.

Try to understand.
이해해 줘.

iaehae jwo.

ee-aha jwo.

Take care of your health.
몸조심 해.

momjosim hae.

mawm-jawseem ha.

Don't cry!
울지 마!

ulji ma!

ooljee mah!

Wipe your tears!
눈물 닦아!

nunmul dakka!

noon-mool dahkk-ah!

Wait for me.
기다려 줘.

gidaryeo jwo.

geedah-ryaw jwo.